May, 2006

Dear Mary,

Few mothers get the joy of seeing their daughters grow into truly great mothers — but I have. I bought this book for you the day Sally turned three. For some reason, it seemed particularly appropriate that day — a true coming of age of the baby. I cannot tell you how much I love and admire what you have done — — as a mother and as a woman, your children are a tribute to your loving, caring ways. May God bless you and your family now and always.

Mom

Moms
ARE A SPECIAL
BLESSING

ARTWORK BY
Jean Monti

HARVEST HOUSE PUBLISHERS

EUGENE, OREGON

Moms Are a Special Blessing
Text Copyright © 2005 by Harvest House Publishers
Eugene, Oregon 97402

ISBN 0-7369-1481-1

Artwork © Jean Monti. It may not be copied or reproduced without permission.
For more information regarding artwork featured in this book, please contact:

Jean Monti
50 Greenfield Rd.
Cumberland, RI 02864
(401) 333-4797

Design and production by Koechel Peterson & Associates, Inc.,
Minneapolis, Minnesota

Harvest House Publishers has made every effort to trace the ownership of all poems and quotes. In
the event of a question arising from the use of a poem or quote, we regret any error made and will
be pleased to make the necessary correction in future editions of this book.

Scripture quotations are taken from the King James Version of the Bible.

Printed in Hong Kong

05 06 07 08 09 10 11 12 / NG / 10 9 8 7 6 5 4 3 2 1

You are such a blessing!

To

Mary Catherine Hohman Zinsner

With love,
Her Mother
Mary Anne Hohman

A MOTHER IS . . .

one who can take the place of all others,
but whose place no one else can take.

GASPARD MERMILLOD

MY MOTHER

HAD A GREAT DEAL

OF TROUBLE WITH ME,

BUT I THINK

SHE ENJOYED IT.

Mark Twain

A *mother is not a person to lean on
but a person to make leaning unnecessary.*

DOROTHY C. FISHER

Mother is the name of God
in the lips and hearts of children.

WILLIAM MAKEPEACE THACKERAY

M   *is for the million things she gave me,*
O   *means only that she's growing old,*
T   *is for the tears she shed to save me,*
H   *is for her heart of purest gold;*
E   *is for her eyes, with love-light shining,*
R   *means right, and right she'll always be,*
Put them all together, they spell "MOTHER,"
A word that means the world to me.

HOWARD JOHNSON

Motherhood:

ALL LOVE BEGINS AND
ENDS THERE.

Robert Browning

*A smart mother makes often a better diagnosis
than a poor doctor.*

AUGUST BIER

ANY MOTHER COULD PERFORM

THE JOBS OF SEVERAL AIR-TRAFFIC

CONTROLLERS WITH EASE.

Lisa Alther

THE HEART OF
A MOTHER IS A
DEEP ABYSS
AT THE BOTTOM OF WHICH
YOU WILL ALWAYS
FIND FORGIVENESS.

Honoré de Balzac

My mother was the most
beautiful woman I ever saw.
All I am I owe to my mother.
I attribute all my success in life to
the moral, intellectual and physical
education I received from her.

GEORGE WASHINGTON

My mother was an angel on earth.
She was a minister of blessing to all human beings
within her sphere of action. She had no feelings but
of kindness and beneficence, yet her mind was as
firm as her temper was mild and gentle.

JOHN QUINCY ADAMS

A man loves his sweetheart the most, his wife the best,
but his mother the longest.

IRISH PROVERB

A MOTHER'S HAPPINESS IS LIKE A

BEACON, LIGHTING UP THE FUTURE

BUT REFLECTED ALSO ON THE PAST

IN THE GUISE OF FOND MEMORIES.

Honoré de Balzac

NO ONE IN THE WORLD

CAN TAKE THE PLACE

 OF YOUR MOTHER.

RIGHT OR WRONG,

FROM HER VIEWPOINT

YOU ARE ALWAYS RIGHT.

SHE MAY SCOLD YOU

FOR LITTLE THINGS,

BUT NEVER

FOR THE BIG ONES.

Harry Truman

HONOUR THY FATHER

AND THY MOTHER,

AS THE LORD THY GOD HATH

COMMANDED THEE;

THAT THY DAYS MAY BE

PROLONGED, AND THAT

IT MAY GO WELL WITH THEE,

IN THE LAND

WHICH THE LORD

THY GOD GIVETH THEE.

The Book of Deuteronomy

She is clothed with strength

and dignity; she can laugh at the days to come.
She speaks with wisdom, and faithful instruction
is on her tongue. She watches over the affairs
of her household and does not eat the bread
of idleness. Her children arise and call her blessed.

THE BOOK OF PROVERBS

WOMEN KNOW

THE WAY TO REAR UP CHILDREN

   (TO BE JUST)

THEY KNOW A SIMPLE, MERRY,

   TENDER KNACK

OF TYING SASHES,

   FITTING BABY SHOES,

AND STRINGING PRETTY WORDS THAT

   MAKE NO SENSE,

AND KISSING FULL SENSE

   INTO EMPTY WORDS.

Elizabeth Barrett Browning

strength

In all my efforts to learn to read,

my mother shared fully my ambition and sympathized

with me and aided me in every way she could.

If I have done anything in life worth attention,

I feel sure that I inherited the

disposition from my mother.

BOOKER T. WASHINGTON

Mommy, I love you
For all that you do.
I'll kiss you and hug you
'Cause you love me, too.
You feed me and need me
To teach you to play,
So smile 'cause I love you
Every single day.

NICOLAS GORDON

15

MOTHER'S ARMS ARE MADE

OF TENDERNESS,

AND SWEET SLEEP BLESSES

THE CHILD WHO LIES THEREIN.

Victor Hugo

A mother is someone who dreams great dreams for you

A mother is someone who dreams great dreams for you, but then she lets you chase the dreams you have for yourself and loves you just the same.

AUTHOR UNKNOWN

A *wonderful being is a mother.*

Other folks may love you, but only your mother understands. Mother works for you, cares for you, loves, and forgives you. And when you leave here, like a guardian angel, her memory is always with you.

AUTHOR UNKNOWN

A MOTHER
is one to whom you hurry
when you are troubled.

EMILY DICKINSON

All-gracious! Grant to those who bear
A mother's charge, the strength and light
To guide the feet that own their care
In ways of Love and Truth and Right.

WILLIAM CULLEN BRYANT

Who ran to help me when I fell,
   And would some pretty story tell,
  Or kiss the place to make it well?
        MY MOTHER.

ANN TAYLOR

They always looked back before turning
the corner, for their mother was always at the
window to nod and smile, and wave her hand to
them. Somehow it seemed as if they couldn't have
got through the day without that, for whatever their
mood might be, the last glimpse of that motherly
face was sure to affect them like sunshine.

LOUISA MAY ALCOTT
Little Women

A MOTHER

UNDERSTANDS

WHAT A CHILD

DOES NOT SAY.

Jewish Proverb

Grace was all in her steps,

Heaven in her eye,

In every gesture

Dignity and love.

JOHN MILTON

ALL MOTHERS ARE

WORKING MOTHERS.

Author Unknown

A mother's love is new every day.
God bless our faithful, good mothers.

ANNE JARVIS

There never was a woman like her.
She was gentle as a dove and brave as a
lioness...The memory of my mother and her
teachings were, after all, the only capital
I had to start life with, and on that
capital I have made my way.

ANDREW JACKSON

IT IS THE MOTHER

WHO CAN CURE

HER CHILD'S TEARS.

African Proverb

Eddie had a sensible mother.
On those nights when he used to come
home nauseated with dealing out chop suey
sundaes and orangeades, and saying that there
was no future for a fellow in our dead little hole,
his mother would give him something rather
special for supper, and set him hoeing and
watering the garden.

EDNA FERBER
Where the Car Turns at 18th

IN VIRTUE ALONE

IS HAPPINESS…

NEVER WAS AN EXISTENCE

UPON EARTH MORE BLESSED

THAN MY MOTHER'S.

John Quincy Adams

I said a Mother's Day prayer

for you to thank the Lord above,

for blessing me with a lifetime

of your tenderhearted love.

I thanked God for the caring

you've shown me through the years,

for the closeness we've enjoyed

in time of laughter and of tears.

And so, I thank you from the heart

for all you've done for me

and I bless the Lord for giving me

the best mother there could be!

AUTHOR UNKNOWN

MY MOTHER WAS THE
SOURCE FROM WHICH
I DERIVED THE
GUIDING PRINCIPLES
OF MY LIFE.
John Wesley

Love is a bridge
that links us heart to heart;
Mother and child
can never live apart.
AUTHOR UNKNOWN

No language can express
the power and beauty and heroism
of a mother's love.
EDWIN CHAPIN

Mother used to sit at the foot of my bed
at night, telling me that I could ask her anything.
When I was a small child, I was certain she could
answer any of my questions. But as I grew older and
my questions became more difficult, that certainty
disappeared and Mother directed me toward God,
who did have all the answers. Oh, I have been
most fortunate to have been blessed with such a mother...

ALDA ELLIS

JUDICIOUS MOTHERS WILL

ALWAYS KEEP IN MIND,

THAT THEY ARE THE FIRST

BOOK READ, AND THE

LAST PUT ASIDE,

IN EVERY CHILD'S LIBRARY.

C. Lenox Redmond

God made a wonderful mother,

A mother who never grows old;

He made her smile of the sunshine,

And He moulded her heart of pure gold;

In her eyes He placed bright shining stars,

In her cheeks fair roses you see;

God made a wonderful mother,

And He gave that dear mother to me.

PAT O'REILLY

If patience is one of the fruits of
the Spirit, then my mother has an orchard of it
growing lushly in her heart.

KIMBERLY MOORE

MEN ARE WHAT
THEIR MOTHERS
MADE THEM.

Ralph Waldo Emerson

Happy is that mother whose ability
to help her children continues on from babyhood
and manhood into maturity. Blessed is the son who
need not leave his mother at the threshold of the
world's activities, but may always and everywhere
have her blessing and her help. Thrice blessed are the
son and the mother between whom there exists an
association not only physical and affectional,
but spiritual and intellectual, and broad
and wise as is the scope of each being.

LYDIA HOYT FARMER

Momma was home.

She was the most totally human,

human being that I have ever known;

and so very beautiful.

She was the lighthouse of her community.

Within our home, she was an abundance of love,

discipline, fun, affection, strength,

tenderness, encouragement,

understanding, inspiration, and support.

Leotyne Price

I *am* still *amazed* at all the things my mother accomplished
when I was a child. She worked a nine-to-five administrative job,
yet still managed to put a hot meal on the table everyday,
including fresh, homebaked goods and desserts, I might add.
On top of this, she ruled a spotless home, sewed clothing for the entire household,
managed to look flawless, and went to bed at a reasonable time.

MICHELLE MCKINNEY HAMMOND

TO DESCRIBE MY MOTHER

WOULD BE TO WRITE ABOUT

A HURRICANE IN ITS

PERFECT POWER.

OR THE CLIMBING, FALLING

COLORS OF A RAINBOW.

Maya Angelou

Of all the special joys in life,
The big ones and the small,
A mother's love and tenderness
Is the greatest of them all.

AUTHOR UNKNOWN

There is no velvet so soft
as a mother's lap, no rose as lovely
as her smile, no path so flowery
as that imprinted with her footsteps.

ARCHIBALD THOMPSON

Reflect on your
present blessings,
of which every man
has many,
not on your past
misfortunes,
of which all
men have some.
CHARLES DICKENS

MY MOTHER HAD A SLENDER,
SMALL BODY, BUT A LARGE
HEART—A HEART SO LARGE
THAT EVERYBODY'S JOYS FOUND
WELCOME IN IT, AND HOSPITABLE
ACCOMMODATION.
Mark Twain

ALL MY MOTHER CAME

INTO MINE EYES

AND GAVE ME UP TO TEARS.

William Shakespeare

Children are the anchors that hold a mother to life.

SOPHOCLES

All that I am or hope to be
I owe to my angel mother. I remember
my mother's prayers and they have
always followed me. They have clung
to me all my life.

ABRAHAM LINCOLN

MOTHERS HOLD THEIR

CHILDREN'S HANDS

FOR A SHORT WHILE,

BUT THEIR HEARTS FOREVER.

Author Unknown